WAITING FOR GODINEZ

ENCRUCIJADAS/CROSSROADS
Santiago Vaquera-Vásquez, Series Editor

Encrucijadas/Crossroads seeks to publish intersectional, trans-American, and transnational Latinx works of fiction, nonfiction, and poetry that build connections between and across the Americas. The series publishes border crossing works that disrupt and destabilize borders. The series will include original books in English, translations that bring important work into English for the first time, and bilingual editions.

Also available in the Encrucijadas/Crossroads:

Dreams in Times of War / Soñar en tiempos de guerra: Stories / Cuentos, An English and Spanish Edition by Oswaldo Estrada

WAITING FOR GODÍNEZ

A TRAGICOMEDY IN TWO ACTS

DANIEL A. OLIVAS

UNIVERSITY OF NEW MEXICO PRESS | ALBUQUERQUE

Library of Congress Cataloging-in-Publication Data
Names: Olivas, Daniel A., author.
Title: Waiting for Godínez: a tragicomedy in two acts / Daniel A. Olivas.
Description: Albuquerque: University of New Mexico Press, 2025. | Series: Encrucijadas = Crossroads
Identifiers: LCCN 2025006769 (print) | LCCN 2025006770 (ebook) | ISBN 9780826368447 (paperback) | ISBN 9780826368454 (epub)
Subjects: LCGFT: Tragicomedies. | Drama.
Classification: LCC PS3615.L58 W35 2025 (print) | LCC PS3615.L58 (ebook) | DDC 812/.6—dc23/eng/20250226
LC record available at https://lccn.loc.gov/2025006769
LC ebook record available at https://lccn.loc.gov/2025006770

Founded in 1889, the University of New Mexico sits on the traditional homelands of the Pueblo of Sandia. The original peoples of New Mexico—Pueblo, Navajo, and Apache—since time immemorial have deep connections to the land and have made significant contributions to the broader community statewide. We honor the land itself and those who remain stewards of this land throughout the generations and also acknowledge our committed relationship to Indigenous peoples. We gratefully recognize our history.

Cover photograph by Olegs Jonins on Unsplash
Designed by Felicia Cedillos
Composed in Adobe Jenson Pro

For my father, Michael Augustine Olivas (1932–2020)

I can't go on. I'll go on.

—Samuel Beckett, *Waiting for Godot*

CONTENTS

PREFACE

Since 1998 I have used fiction to depict and honor my Mexican American experience and culture while challenging the systematic bigotry my community has long suffered. But the anti-immigrant political rhetoric of the 2016 election rose to a level I had never seen in my lifetime. Accordingly, in January 2017 I was inspired to write a fictional response to the presidential election in the form of a dystopian short story in which an unnamed United States president had constructed his long-promised wall at our southern border. His gaudy, gold-embellished structure included an adjoining detention center specifically designed to separate undocumented parents from their US-born children. I convinced my publisher to include this piece in my soon-to-be published story collection in the hopes that my voice would be part of a national outcry against the cruel targeting of immigrants.

But the attacks on our immigrant communities continued and even became normalized in many quarters. So in the summer of 2019, I wanted to go beyond fiction and write a play where—through actors—I could more fully humanize the plight of undocumented immigrants and the harm caused to them by ruthless language and anti-immigrant policies. The result was my first play, *Waiting for Godínez*. Turning to Samuel Beckett's iconic absurdist masterpiece, *Waiting for Godot*, as inspiration for my tale, the forever-waiting characters of Estragon and Vladimir were now embodied in two Mexican friends, Jesús and Isabel. In my play, Immigration and Customs Enforcement agents kidnap Jesús each night and throw him into a cage. But the agents forget to lock the cage, so Jesús escapes and makes his way back to Isabel as they wait for the mysterious Godínez in a city park.

At one point Isabel looks upon her exhausted friend and laments: "What harm have you done to them? You are as much of this country as you are of México. But you are not home in either place. Ni de aquí, ni de allá."

My play struck a nerve. Three Los Angeles theaters produced it in streamed readings in 2020, 2021, and 2022—the pandemic kept us virtual, but the actors and directors in these productions brought my play to life in all its heartbreak and absurdity. A shorter, one-act pandemic version of it was produced for an outdoor stage in the summer of 2021 under the title *Waiting*. In 2023 *Waiting for Godínez* was selected yet again for a play development program and reading, this time with the New York-based Instituto Arte Teatral Internacional (also known as IATI), one of the oldest Latinx theaters in the United States. Finally, in 2024 the venerable Teatro Espejo in Sacramento, California, produced the world premiere of *Waiting for Godínez* for the stage.

Prior to November 2024, I asked myself, how could a play that I wrote in response to the 2016 presidential election still resonate with theaters and audiences? The answer was heartbreakingly simple: We were still witnessing the residual violence done to immigrant families by that administration. Too many children who were separated from their parents and guardians suffered emotional scars. And even with the change in administrations as a result of the 2020 presidential election, immigrant communities still struggled with the unforgiving realities of a dysfunctional immigration system and the vicious politicization of the border. But here we are again with Trump's 2024 return to power based—in large part—on a promise to mobilize Immigration and Customs Enforcement and the military in a mass deportation of immigrants.

Are we all destined to live in a Beckett play as we witness this unending loop of cruelty? In the meantime, undocumented immigrants—many of whom still put themselves at risk doing essential work during our never-ending pandemic—live in legal limbo with a daily fear of being deported.

Ni de aquí, ni de allá.

In *Waiting for Godínez,* an exasperated and bewildered Jesús pleads with his friend Isabel to help him: "I want it to stop. No more cages, no more escaping . . ."

It is indeed time to make such suffering stop. We need humane immigration reform that both acknowledges and respects the tremendous cultural and economic contributions that immigrants bring to the United States. It is my sincere hope that my play, *Waiting for Godínez,* demonstrates the absurdity of doing otherwise while also entertaining and engaging audiences as all worthwhile plays should.

Waiting for Godínez had its world premiere with Teatro Espejo on April 5, 2024, in Sacramento, California, directed by Devin Valdez. Pictured left to right in the foreground: Nicole C. Limón, Lorena Rodríguez, and Ángel Rodríguez. Pictured in back: Pano Roditis. Photograph by Julian Galeano.

PRODUCTION HISTORY

Waiting for Godínez had its world premiere with Teatro Espejo on April 5, 2024, in Sacramento, California, directed by Devin Valdez with the following cast:

JESÚS (CHUY): Ángel Rodríguez
ISABEL (CHAVALITA): Nicole C. Limón
AFORTUNADA: Lorena Rodríguez
PISO: Pano Roditis
CHILD: Santiago Moreno-Colmenares

*

Waiting for Godínez was selected for the Playwrights' Arena Summer Reading Series. It was performed in a streamed reading on July 5, 2020, directed by Dr. Daphnie Sicre with the following cast:

JESÚS (CHUY): Adrian González
ISABEL (CHAVALITA): Sabina Zúñiga Varela
AFORTUNADA: Abigail Marks
PISO: Richard Azurdia
CHILD: Eddie Ruiz
STAGE DIRECTIONS: Diana Burbano

*

Waiting for Godínez was selected for the Road Theatre's Twelfth Annual

Summer Playwrights Festival. It was performed in a streamed reading on July 25, 2021, directed by Sara Guerrero with the following cast:

JESÚS (CHUY): Richard Soto
ISABEL (CHAVALITA): Presciliana Esparolini
AFORTUNADA: Rebecca Bermúdez
PISO: Frank Collison
CHILD: Citlalli "Lalli" Sánchez
STAGE DIRECTIONS: Christine Joëlle

*

Waiting for Godínez was selected for the Garry Marshall Theatre's New Works Festival. It was performed in a streamed reading on September 25, 2022, directed by Dr. Daphnie Sicre with the following cast:

JESÚS (CHUY): Raul Vega Martínez
ISABEL (CHAVALITA): Valentina Guerra
AFORTUNADA: Shanelle Darlene
PISO: Amir Levi
CHILD: Carolina J. Flores
STAGE DIRECTIONS: Mondara Granados Carreiro

*

Waiting for Godínez was selected for the Instituto Arte Teatral Internacional's Cimientos Staged Readings Series. It was performed in a live reading on June 9, 2023, in New York, directed by Andrea Goldman with the following cast:

JESÚS (CHUY): Jesús E. Martínez
ISABEL (CHAVALITA): Gredivel Vásquez
AFORTUNADA: Amy Liou and Svitlana Onopa
PISO: Ilker Öztop
CHILD: Amy Liou and Svitlana Onopa

*

A shorter "pandemic" one-act version of *Waiting for Godínez* was produced under the title *Waiting* in a world premiere on July 24, 2021, in Los Angeles at the Atwater Village Theatre, produced by Playwrights' Arena and directed by Dr. Daphnie Sicre with the following cast:

JESÚS (CHUY): Raul Vega Martínez
ISABEL (CHAVALITA): Valentina Guerra
AFORTUNADA: Shanelle Darlene
PISO: Amir Levi
CHILD: Carolina J. Flores

WAITING FOR GODÍNEZ

CAST OF CHARACTERS

Jesús (also called Chuy): A man. Latino.
Isabel (also called Chavalita): A woman. Latina.
Afortunada: A woman. Any ethnicity.
Piso: A man. Any ethnicity.
Child: Nonbinary. Latinx.

Scene: A park with city skyscrapers in the background.
Time: The present.

ACT I

SETTING: *A moonless evening in a city park. A single tree, with only a few green leaves on its branches, presides over the park, surrounded by lush, green grass. A park bench sits nearby. A dirt path runs in front of the tree and park bench. Off in the horizon we see the silhouette of skyscrapers.*

AT RISE: *JESÚS (also called CHUY), sitting on the park bench, is trying—unsuccessfully—to take off a huarache from his left foot. He wears khaki pants, a white, short-sleeved guayabera, a wristwatch on his left wrist. His clothes are dusty but otherwise neat. He wears no hat. Exhausted, he gives up and, in disgust, drops his left foot onto the grass. ISABEL (also called CHAVALITA)—wearing the same outfit as JESÚS and also dusty—enters, walking stiffly, then stops near JESÚS and leans in to take in the entire scene.*

JESÚS

¡Híjole!

ISABEL

Well said, Chuy. I have often said that, at times, the only proper response to life is "¡híjole!" So I let out a loud "¡híjole!" when life does not go as it should. Sometimes, we have no choice but to yell "¡híjole!" my friend.

(shouting)

"¡Híjole!"

JESÚS

Why are you yelling?

ISABEL

(ISABEL walks to JESÚS, eases down stiffly, sits on the bench.)

Ah! My friend returns. Cuéntame: Where were you last night? I thought I had lost you forever!

JESÚS

I cannot get my pinches huaraches off! They fit yesterday, before I got deported. Now they are cutting through my feet!

ISABEL

Deported, again? Did they beat you?

JESÚS

No of course they did not beat me. They put me into a cage again.

ISABEL

A cage? But you are not a dog.

JESÚS

Are you so sure?

ISABEL

A dog would not wear huaraches.

JESÚS

There is a logic to your argument, Chavalita. I cannot deny that.

ISABEL

And they do not deport dogs, either. Es la verdad. At least, such things are not mentioned in the newspapers. Certainly not the newspapers I read. And my Google searches never lead me to any news about dogs being rounded up and deported. ¡Nunca! Indeed, people just love dogs . . . People everywhere are adopting stray perritos all the time and taking these wretched animals to live in beautiful casas at the beach.

(Imagining pampered dogs, nodding.)

Dogs living like royalty at the beach.

JESÚS

Sí.

ISABEL

Y más: Would a dog wear a shirt?

JESÚS

¡No!

ISABEL

Would a dog wear pants?

JESÚS

¡No!

ISABEL

Would a dog wear a beautiful watch that, though it has stopped, is still correct twice a day?

JESÚS

(Holds up left wrist, looks at his watch, squints at it, holds it up to his ear to listen, shakes his head because he hears nothing, drops hand, stands, smiles.)

My beautiful watch is dead. It was a gift from you, remember? So many years ago. That time we went on vacation in . . . Where was it? Was it in México? We were so young, barely out of our teens. I cannot remember where we went. ¡Dios mío! My yesterdays slip away faster when I try to remember. And the more I forget, the lonelier I feel.

ISABEL

Ni modo. The point is, Chuy, you are not a dog!

(Stands in triumph, slaps JESÚS on shoulder.)

¡Eres una persona, no un animal! You are as much a person as I am, my friend.

JESÚS

But if I were a dog, I would not be deported each night and I would live in a beautiful casa at the beach.

ISABEL

Ah, es la verdad, but you would still be a dog living in a beautiful house at the beach. As the great Mexican poet said: A dog is a dog is a dog.

JESÚS

What do poets know?

ISABEL

Poets understand the mysteries of our existence. And then they write beautiful poems explaining it all to us. Without poets, we would know nothing. Without poets, we would be nothing but animals crawling in the dust.

JESÚS

¿Es cierto?

ISABEL

¡Por supuesto!

JESÚS

So the poets say that we are not dogs?

ISABEL

In so many words.

JESÚS

Do dogs wear hats?

ISABEL

No, dogs do not wear hats.

JESÚS

No hats?

ISABEL

No hats.

JESÚS

(Walks downstage, smiles.)

I do not wear a hat.

ISABEL

(Nods head, walks to JESÚS.)

Sí. You do not even *own* a hat.

JESÚS

I am therefore a dog!

ISABEL

No . . .

JESÚS

And Isabel does not own a hat!

ISABEL

No . . .

JESÚS

And so Isabel is a dog también!

ISABEL

No . . .

JESÚS

¡Los dos somos perritos!

ISABEL

¡No!

JESÚS

(Dejected, remembers that his feet hurt.)

Oh, these huaraches are slicing through my feet.

(Limps back to the bench and sits, cringes in pain.)

Por favor, Chavalita, help me get them off, I beg you. Have mercy on your old friend. We have been friends since we were children. You must help me. ¡Por favor, ayúdame!

ISABEL

(Walks to JESÚS, leans down to look into his face.)

Tell me about the cage.

JESÚS

Oh! They are slicing through my feet!

ISABEL

The cage!

JESÚS

Every night, I get deported, and every day I tell you about the cage!

ISABEL

¡No!

JESÚS

(Shakes, in tears, stands, starts to pace, waving arms.)

¡Sí! Every night! I fall asleep here on this pinche bench, you sleep over there, under that pinche tree, then they come and deport me, throw me into a cage—a cold, horrible, pinche cage fit for a dog—and then I escape because they never lock that pinche cage, and I make my way back to this park, and I always find you snoring over there

(Pointing to tree.)

like a baby, without a care in the world. I crawl back onto this bench, tired, cold, and fall asleep. Then you wake me up, every day. And every day, my feet are swollen, with these pinches huaraches slicing through my skin. ¡Híjole!

ISABEL

How can this be true? I do not remember any of this. Who takes you? Are there many people? Do they have weapons? Do they snarl and abuse you? They must come here silently, like mimes, and slowly lift you from that bench so as not to wake you. Otherwise, I would awake from the noise, I would fight them off, protect you, Chuy!

JESÚS

Every night! Thrown into a cage like a dog, while you sleep under that pinche tree!

ISABEL

But your story makes no sense, Chuy. Once they deport you, why would they put you in a cage? If you are deported, they are free of you, and you are free of them, free to wander in México. No need for a cage.

JESÚS

So there is no cage?

ISABEL

If your story is to make sense, which is what most stories should do, even stories involving you, my old friend, then there is no cage. Unless . . .

JESÚS

Unless what?

ISABEL

Unless they put you in a cage before they try to deport you!

JESÚS

Yes, that must be it!

ISABEL

Makes perfect sense. First the cage, then deportation. We must put the horse before the cart. ¿Sí? Any other way is not logical.

JESÚS

But I trick them! I sneak out and make it back here to be with you so we can wait.

ISABEL

See, I solved the mystery!

JESÚS

Eres brillante, Chavalita.

ISABEL

You are not deported at all!

JESÚS

Es cierto.

ISABEL

Every night, they take you, put you in a cage, but do not deport you, and you always escape because the babosos do not lock the cage. Not so bad, eh? Could be worse . . . Ten men could give you a beating and throw you in that ditch over there every night.

JESÚS

Is that worse than a cold pinche cage?

ISABEL

The beating alone is worse than being thrown in a cage, cold or not.

JESÚS

I suppose that is true.

ISABEL

So, as the famous Mexican playwright said, all's well that ends well.

JESÚS

Who said that?

ISABEL

Names do not matter. The words matter.

JESÚS

(Limps back to bench, sits, gestures to his feet.)

Por favor. Help me with these.

ISABEL

(Walks to JESÚS, bends down, lifts JESÚS's left foot, pulls.)

¡Híjole! Your foot is so swollen, I cannot get this huarache off!

JESÚS

Pull harder!

ISABEL

(Grunts, pulls, and finally yanks off huarache, almost falls on the ground, holds huarache up in triumph.)

Success!

JESÚS

Now the other one!

ISABEL

(Sniffs at huarache, makes a face, tosses it downstage, reaches for the other foot, pulls, grunts, pulls it off in same manner as first.)

Success again!

(Sniffs huarache, makes a face, throws it over to the first one.)

JESÚS

(Wriggling toes, smiling.)

Mucho mejor.

ISABEL

As the great Mexican philosopher said: A friend in need is a friend indeed.

JESÚS

So many Mexicans saying so many things.

ISABEL

Chuy, tell me more about your night away from me.

JESÚS

¿Qué quieres saber?

ISABEL

(Sits beside JESÚS.)

Tell me everything, por favor. From the beginning. Every detail.

JESÚS

(Sighs, stands, limps to tree, thinking, turns to audience, envisions the events he is about to recount. He starts slowly, assuredly, but as his tale continues, he grows more agitated, frightened.)

Last night, you sat under that tree promising to keep watch over me as I slept on this bench. You said, "Chuy, my dear friend, you have nothing to worry about. Te prometo. A promise from me is as good as gold." That is what you say every night: good as gold. So I believed you. Why not? We have been friends since we were little children, and you have never lied to me. Pues, I closed my eyes, I was safe, and sleep came to me. And then it happened: I felt strong hands grab my arms, my legs, my head! These strong men and women—agents—in green uniforms lifted me from the bench. I struggled! I tried to call your name, but nothing came from my mouth. I hoped that you would see what was happening to me! I twisted my head even as one of the agents squeezed it with strong hands. And then I saw you! Asleep, snoring under that pinche tree! A carefree baby! I tried to scream, but my tongue was dead within my mouth. The agents tightened their grip and carried me away. And you snored! They took me to a big black van, threw me in the back with all of these men, women, and children. Los niños estaban llorando. And the agents piled into the front seat and laughed at us. The driver said: "You are going home now." Home! But I was already home, here in this park with you. ¡Contigo! And they drove throughout the night until suddenly we stopped, and an agent opened the back of the van. The other agents pulled us out, one by one, and herded us to a row of small cages. And one by one, they put us each into our own cage, so small I could not stand, I had to crouch. The children kept crying, then their parents started to cry too. And one by one, the agents closed the cages with a loud clang, and they laughed at us. ¿Entiendes? The more we cried, the louder the agents laughed. And as we whimpered, the agents congratulated each other on a good job. Some lit cigarettes. Then slowly they wandered off, laughing, joking, proud of themselves. ¡Qué valientes! Finally we could hear them no longer. And after an hour or so in those cold, dark cages, the others quieted down, and eventually the crying was replaced with soft, sad snoring. The children and their parents, all in their own cages, were tired, and all they could do was sleep. ¡Pero no dormí! I refused to sleep. I needed to come back here, to you, Chavalita. I needed to stay awake and come up with a plan. And then it happened. As I tried to get comfortable, crouching in that cage to plot my escape, I leaned against the cage door, and it fell open! I could not believe my luck! Those babosos forgot to lock my cage! I crept out, on my hands and knees like a baby, and then stood, like a man. I looked at the pobrecitos in their cages, snoring softly, and my heart broke. But what could I do? I have no doubt the agents did not forget to lock *all* of the cages. That would make no sense. So I was the lucky one. I looked around and could not see any of the agents—they were probably drunk someplace, laughing at us, celebrating their great conquest. I crept away, silently into the night, to come back to this park, to this place, my home, to be with you, my friend.

(Sits again, exhausted.)

Esa es toda la historia. And do you know what I thought about as I walked those many miles back to this park? I thought of you, Chavalita. I thought of your face, your voice, your embrace. That is what kept me walking, step by step, mile after mile. The thought of you. But I also had other thoughts. Tenía preguntas. Such as: Why do you lie to me? You make promises to protect me, but you do not. And that means you lie to me, each day, every day. ¿Me estás escuchando?

ISABEL

Oh, Chuy, that story is unbelievable! How can any of this be true? You know I would always protect you, even from a horde of agents with strong hands. You must be dreaming. My word is as good as gold, I have told you. I would never lie to you. ¿Entiendes? If agents ever tried to touch you, I would fight them off!

JESÚS

¡Cada noche!

ISABEL

Oh, Chuy, lo siento. I know you would not lie to me. If you say it happens every night, it happens every night.

JESÚS

(calmer, sighing)

Cada noche.

ISABEL

(soothingly)

Sí, Chuy. Cada noche.

JESÚS

Chavalita, I want it to stop. No more cages, no more escaping, no more swollen feet. Ya basta.

ISABEL

Your pain is never ending, eh?

JESÚS

Sí.

ISABEL

Just like Sisyphus.

JESÚS

(Scratches groin.)

I had a bad case of that when I was younger. But I have fond memories of the lovely lady who gave it to me.

ISABEL

¡No, tonto! I said: Sisyphus! SI-SY-PHUS!

JESÚS

¿Sisy-quién?

ISABEL

From Greek mythology, Chuy. Sisyphus. You know, that poor pendejo who was punished by the gods and forced to roll a huge boulder up a hill, and each time he gets to the top of the hill, the pinche boulder rolls down. And he starts again, pushing that boulder up the hill. You are just like him, but your rock is not a rock at all, but a cage.

JESÚS

Ah! You are right. He is a pendejo. If I were him, I would stop pushing that boulder up the hill and go far away, someplace else, away from that boulder and that hill, someplace where I could take a long nap.

(yawning)

I am so tired. I never close my eyes—not even for a minute—when I am in that cold cage. And then all those miles walking back to you. I want to go someplace else and sleep, far from here, where they cannot find me.

ISABEL

But we cannot go someplace else. Godínez told us to wait for him here by this tree.

JESÚS

Godínez? Are you sure? Can Godínez save me from the agents and that cold cage? Is that why we are here to meet him?

ISABEL

I cannot remember. I texted a note to myself, I think.

(Stands, pulls out cellphone from pants pocket, looks at it, shakes it, sighs.)

My battery is dead.

(Puts cellphone back in pocket, sits again.)

JESÚS

(Stands, limps to tree, looks up into tree's branches.)

I wonder what kind of tree this is. I wonder if in the old days, this was a hanging tree. A tree that could bring sleep. With a bit of rope.

(Thinks, searches pockets for rope, comes up empty, shrugs, looks back up at tree.)

It would be so easy. Sí. Muy fácil. Maybe Godínez is up there watching us.

ISABEL

(Stands, walks to JESÚS, looks up into branches.)

No, they say Godínez is an older gentleman who was once lean but has grown quite corpulent with age. I do not think he could scramble up this tree.

(Walks back to the bench, sits.)

JESÚS

Why was he lean?

ISABEL

They say he was a famous bicyclist, raced once in the Tour de France.

JESÚS

They have the Eiffel Tower in France.

ISABEL

Sí.

JESÚS

But I have not seen it, except in photos, of course.

(ISABEL nods in agreement.)

And there is that beautiful plaque at the bottom of the Eiffel Tower . . .

(ISABEL stops nodding, turns to JESÚS in anticipation for what he will say next.)

You know the words—hermosas palabras—on that plaque:

(Puts right hand on heart to recite the words solemnly.)

"Give me your tired, your poor / Your huddled masses yearning to breathe free . . ."

ISABEL

¡No, idiota! That plaque is *not* on the Eiffel Tower!

JESÚS

But I saw it on the internet. The internet does not lie.

ISABEL

¡No! That is not where you saw those words, Chuy.

JESÚS

I did not see them on the internet?

ISABEL

¡Quién sabe! You might have seen those words on the internet, but not on the Eiffel Tower. Or maybe you dreamed them. Perhaps they are on the dollar bill.

(Searching pockets unsuccessfully for a dollar.)

Godínez would know. He knows money, and he bicycled in France.

JESÚS

But they are such pretty words.

ISABEL

Do not trust pretty words.

JESÚS

But words matter.

ISABEL

Words matter, until they do not.

JESÚS

Oh, tell me more about Godínez!

ISABEL

They say he is a total pelón. Not a hair on his head, even when he was younger.

JESÚS

(Returns to bench, sits next to ISABEL.)

And now?

ISABEL

Still bald.

JESÚS

¡No! What does Godínez do now that he is too old and fat to race?

ISABEL

He owns a bicycle repair shop, of course.

JESÚS

Claro que sí.

ISABEL

And he told us to wait here by this tree.

JESÚS

What kind of tree is it? Is it a hanging tree?

ISABEL

(Shrugs, pensive.)

This tree will die.

JESÚS

Sí.

ISABEL

This grass will die.

JESÚS

Sí.

ISABEL

I will die.

JESÚS

Sí.

ISABEL

You will die.

(silence)

You will die.

(Silence, turns to JESÚS, who avoids ISABEL's eyes.)

You will die.

(silence)

I will die.

JESÚS

Sí.

ISABEL

(sighs)

JESÚS

Perhaps Godínez will help me so that I will not be snatched up again and thrown in a cold cage like a dog.

ISABEL

Perhaps. They say Godínez does good deeds by employing people at the bicycle shop who cannot find employment elsewhere. So we know he is capable of helping others. ¿Me entiendes? Yet people also say that Godínez beats one of the two children who works for him. The other child he does not bother, for some reason. So I have been told. They are brother and sister, twins. I do not know where they came from—who their parents are. They must be orphans. You remember them, do you not? We have seen them playing in the park on many occasions. One of them—I am not certain which—came to us that one day—was it Tuesday?—to say that we should wait for Godínez by this tree. I believe Godínez is to come today. I am certain my text to myself would confirm this, but alas the battery is dead so I cannot check. So we have no choice but to wait.

JESÚS

Perhaps Godínez will save me from the cold cage.

ISABEL

Perhaps.

JESÚS

(Rubbing stomach.)

Tengo hambre. Do you have any mangos left?

ISABEL

(Feeling about in her pockets.)

No. You ate the last one yesterday.

JESÚS

I will even take a limón, Chavalita.

ISABEL

No, I have nothing. You have eaten them all. Not one mango, not one limón. There is nothing left. ¡Nada!

JESÚS

Tengo hambre.

(yawning)

Estoy cansado.

(Shaking head, blinking.)

But I must stay awake.

ISABEL

Then let us talk of things.

JESÚS

¿Qué cosas?

ISABEL

(Thinking for a moment.)

Ah! We need a story!

JESÚS

¡Sí! ¡Un cuento!

ISABEL

You begin!

JESÚS

Not about that pinche cage again!

ISABEL

¡No! A happy story! One with great adventure.

JESÚS

¡Sí!

ISABEL

How about one from the Bible!

JESÚS

(Stands, walks to center stage, gets ready to tell a story.)

¡Sí! ¡La Biblia!

ISABEL

Make it a good one!

JESÚS

¡Por supuesto!

ISABEL

Which story?

JESÚS

¡Daniel en el foso de los leones!

ISABEL

I love this one! Poor Daniel! I can imagine those hungry lions smacking their lips.

JESÚS

Who is telling this story?

ISABEL

Lo siento. Continue, Chuy. I will be quiet. But make it good!

JESÚS

Por supuesto. All of the Bible stories are exciting, except for the begats.

(Clears throat to prepare.)

Once upon a time, there were two amigos named Daniel and Darius. Daniel was very holy—un santo! And Darius was a very rich man with great power, a mansion, and many things that made him happy. But Daniel was his best friend who made him happier than all the gold in the world. Pues, there were others who were very jealous of this friendship. Esos idiotas celosos cooked up a plan. They got Darius to sign some papers—I do not know what kind of papers—no soy abogado. But because of these papers, poor Daniel was thrown into a den of lions just because he was who he was. Nada más. When Darius found out he was tricked, he cried and he cried. The same way I would cry if I did una cosa estupida that turned you into dinner for some hungry cats. So Darius ran as fast as his legs could take him to that den of lions.

ISABEL

What happened?

JESÚS

No pasó nada. When Darius got to the den, he found Daniel standing safely outside the den.

ISABEL

How did he escape?

JESÚS

Pues, Daniel had another amigo named Jacob who always carried a big ladder with him wherever he went, because you never know when someone might need a ladder. ¿Entiendes? Jacob looked down into the lions' den and saw his poor amigo about to be eaten by six lions! So, thinking fast, Jacob lowered his wonderful ladder down into the den. And this ladder was special! It was surrounded by angels! These beautiful angelitos helped Daniel get onto the ladder, and up he scrambled to safety.

ISABEL

What?

JESÚS

(Struts over triumphantly and sits on the bench near ISABEL.)

The end.

ISABEL

No, something is wrong. Daniel did not escape with the help of Jacob's ladder.

JESÚS

Está en la Biblia.

ISABEL

No—yes—no—I mean, both stories are in the Bible. You have made two into one.

JESÚS

And that is what we call a miracle!

ISABEL

No.

JESÚS

La Biblia está llena de milagros.

ISABEL

(Perks up.)

What is that? ¿Quién está ahí?

(Looks stage right, searching for someone.)

Could that be Godínez?

PISO

(off)

You lazy creature! Pull faster! I have places to be! Time slips away and it shall never return!

ISABEL

¡Ay, Dios mío!

(ISABEL jumps up, hides behind the park bench, clutches the back of the bench, and crouches, peering over the bench back. JESÚS notices ISABEL is hiding, jumps up and joins her, crouches.)

PISO

(off)

Faster!

(PISO and AFORTUNADA enter stage right. AFORTUNADA pulls a large, two-wheeled, rickety wooden cart that is painted in faded colors. In the cart sits PISO in a wing-backed, beat-up upholstered chair, holding a glass of wine. They both wear the same outfit: black pants and black, short-sleeved guayaberas, but PISO's clothes are clean, while AFORTUNADA's clothes are dusty. PISO's hair is white from age but nicely cut and combed. He is

a hearty man. AFORTUNADA's hair is unkempt. AFORTUNADA pulls the cart to center stage. ISABEL and JESÚS watch in alarm from behind the park bench.)

It is time to rest. Stop here!

(AFORTUNADA stops suddenly and drops the cart's handles, making PISO lose his balance and spill wine on his pants, which he wipes dramatically with his free hand.)

Imbecile!

(AFORTUNADA looks down, ashamed and afraid. PISO stands.)

Open!

(AFORTUNADA shuffles to the little gate at the side of the cart, opens it, waits.)

Stepstool!

(AFORTUNADA jumps, reaches into the cart, pulls out a stepstool, places it in front of the cart's door. PISO gingerly steps out of the cart, holding wineglass aloft to avoid spilling again, steps onto the ground triumphantly. PISO preens, examines his clothing, brushing off nonexistent dust. Examines the wineglass, drinks the last of the wine, smacks his lips, hands empty wineglass to AFORTUNADA, who gingerly puts wineglass into the cart.)

ISABEL

(Pops up from behind bench.)

Is that him?

JESÚS

(Pops up from behind bench.)

Who?

ISABEL

You know . . .

JESÚS

I do not remember . . .

ISABEL

Godínez!

JESÚS

¿Quién?

ISABEL

Godínez!

JESÚS

Sí, sí, it must be Godínez. We are waiting for him, correct?

ISABEL

¡Sí!

JESÚS

¡Magnífico!

ISABEL

¡Estupendo!

JESÚS

¡Brillante!

ISABEL

¡Guapo!

JESÚS

¡Un genio!

(JESÚS jumps out from behind the park bench, runs toward PISO. ISABEL follows closely behind. They stop in front of PISO, who looks them up and down.)

Señor Godínez!

(Opens arms, hoping to embrace.)

PISO

(Steps back, a little frightened.)

Who? What?

ISABEL

What my friend meant to say was: Welcome, Señor Godínez! We have been waiting for you as you requested.

PISO

I do not know this Señor . . . Cortés of whom you speak.

JESÚS

¡No! Not Cortés! Godínez! You do not know your own name?

PISO

(Gaining composure, extends his right hand to JESÚS. JESÚS smiles, takes PISO's hand, and they start to shake hands slowly.)

My name is Piso . . .

JESÚS

(JESÚS's smile disappears, pulls hand away.)

Piso? That is a low name!

PISO

(Puzzled, tries again, this time extending his hand to ISABEL, who takes his hand, and they start to shake.)

At your service. I am Señor Piso Mojado.

(ISABEL drops PISO's hand, turns to JESÚS. They stare at each other in amazement, start to laugh.)

ISABEL

(laughing)

Piso Mojado?

PISO

You laugh, but my name is seen in thousands of hotels and luxurious office buildings across the country.

JESÚS

(laughing)

Wherever there are dirty floors to mop!

(JESÚS and ISABEL convulse in laughter.)

PISO

(Insulted, determined to impress.)

Gentlepeople, as I said, I am Piso Mojado, not Cortés or García or . . . Godínez. You may call me Piso. At your service.

(Reaches for his hat to tip but realizes he is not wearing a hat, shakes his head, bows dramatically instead.)

ISABEL

Not Godínez. The joke is on us, eh, Chuy? Nothing matters . . . again.

JESÚS

Sí. Nada importa. Una vez más.

ISABEL

And what are you famous for?

JESÚS

Are you more famous than Godínez?

PISO

I do not know this Godínez of whom you speak. So perhaps I am more famous than he. We call that logic.

ISABEL

And what are you famous for?

JESÚS

Are you more famous than Godínez?

PISO

Gentlepeople, I heard you the first time. My fame comes from the work of others, which makes me a genius.

JESÚS

(Excited, smiles proudly, nudges ISABEL.)

I told you, Chavalita! ¡Un genio!

ISABEL

What is it that you do?

PISO

(Bows deeply, slowly stands erect, proud.)

I am a literary agent. My business card.

(Pulls out small business cards from his pants pocket, hands one each to ISABEL and JESÚS, who examine the cards closely. ISABEL holds the card below her chest to look at it. JESÚS holds it up toward the sky to examine his.)

ISABEL

(reading card)

"Señor Piso Mojado. Literary agent of the highest regard and standards."

JESÚS

(reading card)

"Representing only the most talented creators of poetry, fiction, histories, and memoirs."

ISABEL

(reading card)

"Only the finest representation of the greatest authors of our time."

(PISO puffs out chest, puts hands on hips, looks out toward audience, proudly.)

JESÚS

(reading card)

"Manuscript submission guidelines: Please send your queries in the body of an email; no attachments please."

ISABEL

(reading card)

"Emails with attachments shall not be read and shall be deleted immediately."

(PISO nods seriously.)

JESÚS

(reading card)

"Follow me on Twitter, Instagram, and LinkedIn."

ISABEL

(Turns to PISO, puzzled.)

LinkedIn?

PISO

I cast a wide net. Even nerds write bestsellers.

ISABEL

(Turns to JESÚS, nods.)

He is a genius.

PISO

(PISO snatches the business cards from ISABEL and JESÚS, puts them back into his pants pocket. JESÚS and ISABEL stare at their empty hands, mouths open, startled.)

Printing and paper costs are up, gentlepeople, so I must conserve where I can.

AFORTUNADA

(shouting)

Anaphora!

(Startled, ISABEL and JESÚS run back to park bench, sit, and hold each other in fear.)

Couplet!

(ISABEL and JESÚS shake in fear, hug each tighter.)

Enjambment!
Meter!
Epigraph!
Dactyl!

(pauses for emphasis)

Stanza!

PISO

(Puts hand on AFORTUNADA's shoulder, sternly.)

Enough!

AFORTUNADA

(Turns to PISO, uncertain, whispers.)

Quatrain?

PISO

I said enough!

(Removes hand from AFORTUNADA's shoulder, struts over to ISABEL and JESÚS.)

No need to be afraid, gentlepeople.

ISABEL

Who is that?

JESÚS

Your slave?

PISO

Oh, no, no. Slavery was outlawed long ago. Afortunada is a poet, one of my clients, who had shown great promise at one time . . . She did a residency at Yaddo, had poems published in the finest literary journals, anthologized by the most reputable publishers, a debut collection that received several glowing reviews. But, alas . . .

ISABEL AND JESÚS

(Standing, no longer frightened but curious.)

Alas what?

PISO

(Sighing, walks over to AFORTUNADA, looks her up and down, shakes his head.)

Alas, even the most successful and talented poet can make nothing more than a mere pittance . . . not enough money to keep one fed and clothed. A "bestselling"

(Gesturing air quotes.)

poetry collection might sell a thousand copies, if you are lucky. So, gentlepeople, I am taking this poor wretch of a poet to the city to exchange her for a novelist who, as we all know, can sell hundreds of thousands of books and even have Hollywood option his or her work to be made into a blockbuster film. Yes, that is where the money sits, just waiting for me—and my client—to benefit from. Hollywood blockbuster! As we all know, poets may sound quite pretty, but their words mean nothing and, worse yet, poets do not create a steady and substantial income flow. Yes, for reasons that I cannot fathom, everyone wants to be a poet. The world is lousy with poets, crammed with poets, bloated with poets.

And that, gentlepeople, is the greatest tragedy humankind has ever known. Poets are a pestilence for which there is no treatment, no inoculation, no vaccine. And sadly I learned that lesson quite late in life.

(Walking back to ISABEL and JESÚS.)

So you see, gentlepeople, I must drop this client, this poet, and find a novelist to add to my list. It must be done. I have no choice, or else I will starve from the measly percentage I am paid from Afortunada's meager royalties.

ISABEL

(Moving closer to AFORTUNADA, looks her up and down.)

But is her poetry not good?

PISO

Au contraire! She is one of the great poets of our time! But who buys poetry? Who listens to poetry? Who cares about poetry? No one except for the poets who want to see their pretty words in print. That is why I must exchange my poet for a novelist. Everyone reads novels, or at least they say they do. But the key is this: People buy novels even if they do not read them. Thousands and thousands of books are purchased by the public each day, and agents can eat well and wear the finest clothing.

JESÚS

(Joining ISABEL and PISO.)

¡Quiero escuchar un poema!

ISABEL

Yes! That would be a pretty way to spend time as we wait for Godínez!

JESÚS

(Turning to ISABEL.)

Who is Godínez?

ISABEL

(Hitting JESÚS's shoulder.)

We are waiting for Godínez!

JESÚS

(Rubbing his shoulder.)

Sí, sí. Estamos esperando a Godínez.

PISO

Yes, yes, we may have my poet recite a few pretty words. Why not? She will not be with me much longer, so I might as well get some use out of her, even if it is just to entertain two strangers. But before we proceed, I have a question, just so I can situate myself, as it were. To whom am I speaking?

ISABEL

I am Isabel, but my friends call me Chavalita. And he is Jesús, but his friends call him Chuy.

PISO

But who are you to each other?

ISABEL AND JESÚS

(Extremely puzzled.)

What do you mean?

PISO

Put another way, what is your relationship?

(All three stare at each other in silence until it becomes very uncomfortable.)

ISABEL

We are . . .

JESÚS

That is to say . . .

ISABEL

There is some history . . .

JESÚS

Sí. Algo de historia . . .

ISABEL

That I cannot quite remember right now . . .

JESÚS

Sí, hay una historia que yo tampoco recuerdo.

(All three stare at each other in silence until it again becomes very uncomfortable.)

PISO

Yes, yes, well, never mind. We all have things we cannot remember or that we make a great effort to forget. And besides, I think I am as situated as I will ever be with the two of you. So let us have my poet recite a few pretty words as we take a little rest from our travels.

(Pointing to stepstool.)

Afortunada, prepare to orate!

(AFORTUNADA steps onto the stool, faces audience, clears throat.)

Recite the poem "Sisyphus Explains."

JESÚS

(upset)

Sisyphus? Again?

PISO

She has not recited this for you before.

ISABEL

Ni modo. Ignore Chuy. Let us hear the poem.

PISO

Very well.

ISABEL

Before she starts, one question.

PISO

Yes?

ISABEL

Did she write this poem?

PISO

No, this is not one of her compositions. If she read one of her own poems, I would have to charge you royalties so that I could get my appropriate percentage of the proceeds. But I assume, gentlepeople, you do not have a dime between you.

(ISABEL and JESÚS search their pockets, come up empty, look at PISO in embarrassment.)

I thought so. This poem is by another poet, not one of my clients, so I do not care if I violate his copyright. Besides, he is a minor poet, and certainly not one who can afford to hire an attorney to sue me for violation of his intellectual property.

(Turning to AFORTUNADA.)

Please, recite "Sisyphus Explains."

AFORTUNADA

(Clears throat, holds up right index finger, recites in dramatic voice.)

Sisyphus Explains. A poem.
They laugh
or cry
at my "plight"
that I need not
describe.
But, in truth,
this is great pleasure
for me, nothing less.
I am known for
my grand cunning,
great hubris, and
ferocious thirst
for power.
But this hill,
this stone,
this eternal
toil are all part
of my plan.
Tartarus is hilly
and charming, far
from my petty
concerns in Corinth.
So I am free to ponder
life's great mysteries
as I repeat my simple
and predictable

employment.
Do not cry for me,
Glaucus, Ornytion,
Thersander, and Almus.
Treat each other well,
my sons, and
know that I am
at peace,
that I am well.

(Drops right arm, steps off stool, bows head, waits.)

ISABEL

(Smiling, clapping.)

Wonderful!

JESÚS

(Smiling, clapping.)

¡Otro poema!

ISABEL

(Smile disappears, clapping slows, stops, suddenly pensive.)

But what did it mean?

JESÚS

(Smile disappears, clapping slows, stops, also suddenly pensive.)

Yes, what did it mean?

PISO

Does it matter? They are just words organized into lines and stanzas. Why should it mean anything?

ISABEL AND JESÚS

(ISABEL and JESÚS look at each other, shrug, turn back to PISO. They smile, excited again.)

Another poem, please!

PISO

Not another poem!

ISABEL AND JESÚS

(Clapping, in unison.)

¡Otro! ¡Otro! ¡Otro!

PISO

No!

JESÚS

Quiero un poema sobre gatos.

PISO

What? You want a poem about . . . cats?

ISABEL

(Turning to JESÚS.)

Chuy, you have never owned a cat.

JESÚS

No one really ever *owns* a cat.

ISABEL

Es cierto.

JESÚS

But if I owned a cat, I would name him Nacho.

ISABEL

(Thinking, trying to remember something, eventually giving up.)

A fine name. A name I know, I believe. But I cannot remember where I know it from. Ni modo. Ni modo.

(Turning back to PISO.)

How about a cat poem?

PISO

No!

(Turning to audience.)

No one ever made any money from cat poems.

JESÚS

(To PISO.)

Do you have a mango or even a limón?

(Rubbing stomach.)

Tengo mucha hambre.

PISO

(Turning, stepping onto stool and into cart.)

No time for mangos, gentlepeople, though I have many here in this lunch basket.

JESÚS

(distraught)

¡No!

PISO

Off to the city for a novelist! Afortunada, get back to your post and pull as if it matters to you!

(AFORTUNADA gets in front of cart, grabs handles, and starts to pull.)

PISO

Adieu, gentlepeople! We will never see each other again, no doubt, but wish me well in my endeavors. Faster, Afortunada! Faster!

(PISO and AFORTUNADA exit. ISABEL and JESÚS follow them slowly, sadly.)

PISO

Faster!

(off)

Faster, I say!

ISABEL

They are gone forever.

JESÚS

And so are the mangos.

(yawning)

Estoy tan cansado.

(Climbing onto bench, curls up to nap, facing audience, closes eyes.)

Let me sleep.

ISABEL

Again?

JESÚS

I never can sleep. Please give me some peace. No te pido mucho.

ISABEL

(relenting)

Sleep, my old friend. Rest so that we will be ready to meet Godínez. He should be here, perhaps while you sleep, dear friend . . . but do not worry, I shall awaken you. But sleep for now. Sleeping is the best way to wait. Indeed, sleeping is the best way to live.

CHILD

(off)

Mr. Albert?

(entering stage right)

Mr. Albert?

(Stopping in front of ISABEL, who looks down at CHILD.)

ISABEL

Why do you call me Mr. Albert?

CHILD

Are you Mr. Albert?

ISABEL

I am Isabel. But you may call me Señora Soledad out of respect for my age and station. Who is it you are looking for? Are you the child who came Tuesday with the news that Señor Godínez wanted us to wait for him by this tree?

CHILD

No, Señora Soledad. That was not me. Maybe it was my twin.

ISABEL

Ah! You are one of the twins, yes? You both work at the bicycle repair shop for Señor Godínez, correct?

CHILD

Sí, Señora Soledad.

ISABEL

Which one are you?

CHILD

What do you mean, Señora Soledad?

ISABEL

Are you the boy or the girl?

CHILD

I do not know, Señora Soledad.

ISABEL

You must know.

CHILD

No, Señora Soledad.

ISABEL

Ni modo. Does Señor Godínez beat you or your twin?

CHILD

He beats my twin, Señora Soledad.

ISABEL

Ah! So perhaps you are the girl? Maybe Señor Godínez is a man of the old ways and would only beat a boy?

CHILD

I do not know, Señora Soledad.

ISABEL

(pause)

Look at my face.

CHILD

(Puzzled, then complies.)

Sí, Señora Soledad.

ISABEL

(Turns face slowly from side to side so the CHILD can get a good look, stops turning face, looks into CHILD's eyes, searching for the truth.)

Do you recognize me?

CHILD

No, Señora Soledad.

ISABEL

Are you certain?

CHILD

Sí, Señora Soledad.

ISABEL

(Sternly, as a parent would speak.)

You would not lie to me, child.

CHILD

(A little frightened.)

No, Señora Soledad.

ISABEL

(Satisfied, thinking in silence, then gets an idea.)

You are very thin. Are you hungry, child?

CHILD

Sí, Señora Soledad.

ISABEL

(Searching pockets, finds mango, presents it to CHILD.)

Here, child, a delicious, ripe mango for you. Take it.

CHILD

(Taking mango in both hands.)

Gracias, Señora Soledad.

ISABEL

And do you have a message for me from Señor Godínez?

CHILD

Sí, Señora Soledad.

ISABEL

And what is that message?

CHILD

Señor Godínez says that he cannot come this evening, but he hopes to come tomorrow.

ISABEL

But we have waited all day for him, child. What of that? Does that matter?

CHILD

I do not know, Señora Soledad.

ISABEL

(sighs)

Well, tomorrow it must be. We have no choice, do we? You may go now, child.

CHILD

But Señora Soledad . . .

ISABEL

What is it, child?

CHILD

What should I tell Señor Godínez?

ISABEL

Tell him you met me, we spoke, I fed you, and I sent you off. Can you do that, child?

CHILD

Sí, Señora Soledad.

(CHILD hesitates, turns, starts to walk, turns to look at ISABEL one last time as if to say something, thinks better of it, then runs off. Suddenly, sky goes dark. It is now a dark night. Moon rises into the middle of the night sky.)

ISABEL

(ISABEL addresses the moon.)

You have returned, my old friend. Just in time. I have so much to tell you. My days are filled with so much . . . Oh, I cannot remember. But they are filled with many things that I want to share with you. If you have but a moment, I can gather my memories, and I will tell you everything.

JESÚS

(Stirring, eyes still closed.)

Chavalita? ¿Dónde estás?

ISABEL

(Looks toward JESÚS, starts to walk to him.)

Estoy aquí.

(Standing in front of bench, looking down.)

Estoy aquí, Chuy.

(Bending over, ISABEL lifts JESÚS's head, sits, gingerly puts JESÚS's head on her lap.)

JESÚS

(Eyes still closed, sighing.)

Do not let them take me again, Chavalita. I do not want to be put in that cold cage ever again. Stay here, por favor.

ISABEL

(Slowly patting JESÚS's arm to soothe him.)

I will protect you, Chuy. I will keep you safe. I will not sleep under the tree this time. I will stay here, near you and alert all night. Do not worry, my old friend. I will never betray you.

JESÚS

(Sighing, peacefully.)

Mil gracias.

ISABEL

Por nada.

JESÚS

Tengo hambre. Do you have a mango?

ISABEL

No, Chuy. I gave you the last one yesterday.

JESÚS

Oh, yes, you said that.

ISABEL

But maybe tomorrow I will have a mango. And I promise to give it to you.

JESÚS

Sí. Mañana.

ISABEL

In the meantime, I will stay alert.

JESÚS

Gracias, Chavalita.

ISABEL

I will protect you.

JESÚS

Gracias, Chavalita.

ISABEL

No one will take you tonight.

JESÚS

Gracias, Chavalita.

ISABEL

I have always taken care of you, my friend. I will continue to do so until our last days on earth.

JESÚS

Gracias, Chavalita.

ISABEL

I cannot imagine a world without you.

JESÚS

Gracias, Chavalita.

ISABEL

You are my friend.

JESÚS

Gracias, Chavalita.

ISABEL

You may trust me.

JESÚS

Gracias, Chavalita.

ISABEL

Te prometo. A promise from me is as good as gold.

JESÚS

Gracias, Chavalita.

(Both grow quiet. ISABEL's eyes start to flutter. She slowly nods off. Both are now asleep. Tableau.)

(CURTAIN, END OF ACT I.)

ACT II

SETTING: *Next day. Same city park, a moonless evening. Silhouette of skyscrapers off in the horizon. Scene is identical to Act I, except all of the leaves from the tree have fallen, scattered about the grass and road. The park is empty. JESÚS's huaraches sit near the bench as they were the night before.*

AT RISE: *Enter ISABEL, strolling, hands in pockets. Stops in front of tree. Scratches head, puzzled. Looks down, sees leaves. Picks up one leaf, examines it, lets it fall back to ground. Looks over to bench, turns, strolls to bench, examines it, looks around the park, sees no one, sits down, remains silent for several moments taking in scene.*

ISABEL

(whispering)

Híjole.

(Remains silent, looking around the park. Finally ISABEL stands, looks down to examine bench, looks around park to make certain no one else is around, climbs onto bench, faces audience, stands erect, raises right index finger, clears throat.)

Sisyphus Explains. A poem.
They laugh
or cry
at my "plight"

that I need not
describe.
But, in truth,
this is great pleasure
for me, nothing less.
I am known for
my grand cunning,
great hubris, and
ferocious thirst
for power.
But this hill,
this stone,
this eternal
toil are all part
of my plan.
Tartarus is hilly
and charming, far
from my petty
concerns in Corinth.
So I am free to ponder
life's great mysteries
as I repeat my simple
and predictable
employment.
Do not cry for me,
Glaucus, Ornytion,
Thersander, and Almus.
Treat each other well,
my sons, and
know that I am
at peace,
that I am well.

(ISABEL smiles, bows, drops right arm, steps off bench, sits again. Hears someone coming. Enter JESÚS walk-

ing slowly, barefoot. He approaches ISABEL, stops in front of ISABEL, turns, walks over to tree, looks up into the barren branches, looks down at the leaves strewn about, slowly bends and picks up one leaf, examines it curiously, shrugs, drops leaf, turns, walks to bench, sits, sighs, sees his huaraches, slips them on one at a time.)

ISABEL

You again.

JESÚS

Sí, soy yo otra vez.

ISABEL

Where have you been? I thought I had lost you forever.

JESÚS

We have been friends for many years, since we were niños pequeños.

ISABEL

(Ignoring JESÚS's observation.)

Where have you been? I thought I had lost you forever.

JESÚS

(Calmly, resigned to his recurring plight.)

They took me last night, while you snored like a baby . . . They took me, threw me into that cold cage. But I escaped before they could deport me. The babosos forgot to lock the pinche cage again, so I escaped, and walked miles with no huaraches on my feet, back to here.

ISABEL

I am always here for you.

JESÚS

That is the problem.

ISABEL

You are cruel.

JESÚS

You are here.

ISABEL

If you needed my help, why did you not cry out?

JESÚS

Why did you not listen?

ISABEL

There is nothing wrong with my ears.

JESÚS

That makes it worse.

ISABEL

¡Idiota!

JESÚS

¡Tonta!

ISABEL

¡Pendejo!

JESÚS

¡Ingrata!

ISABEL

¡Monstruo!

JESÚS

¡Chupacabra!

ISABEL

¡Asesino!

JESÚS

¡La Llorona!

ISABEL

¡Diablo!

JESÚS

(with finality)

¡Abogada!

ISABEL

¡Ay!

(She wilts, vanquished.)

JESÚS

Credo quia absurdum est.

ISABEL

What?

JESÚS

That is Latin.

ISABEL

You speak Latin?

JESÚS

Por supuesto. Soy Latino.

ISABEL

(Fed up, ISABEL stands, walks over to tree, examines tree's empty branches, puzzled by what she sees, shakes her head in confusion, finally lets out a sigh.)

This looks different from yesterday.

JESÚS

Es lo mismo.

ISABEL

No, it is different. Somehow. I cannot remember.

(Grabbing head with both hands.)

But I know it is different.

(Dropping hands to side, shaking head.)

It is different from yesterday.

JESÚS

Es lo mismo.

ISABEL

(Walking back to bench, sits.)

Why did you leave me last night?

JESÚS

(Irritated, voice rising.)

Ya te dije lo que pasó. The agents came, in green uniforms, grabbed me with their big hands, and threw me in that black van with all the others. I can still hear their cries, especially los niños! And then, after driving through the night, those agents threw us all into those pinches cages, but they forgot to lock mine, so I escaped, and I left all the others behind, locked in their cages, snoring. I walked all night. And now I am here.

(sighs)

But these new huaraches fit my swollen feet better than my old ones. That is one good thing.

ISABEL

No, those are your old huaraches. Remember, I helped you take them off, and we put them here yesterday by the bench. They have not moved. They are your old huaraches.

JESÚS

My old huaraches were a lighter brown. These are dark brown. I wonder who left them here? He clearly has larger feet than I.

ISABEL

Did you miss me?

JESÚS

When?

ISABEL

When you were in that cage last night.

JESÚS

I always miss you, even when I am with you.

ISABEL

I do not know if that makes me very happy.

JESÚS

No es mi trabajo hacerte feliz.

ISABEL

(sighs)

I just want happy days.

JESÚS

I just want happy nights.

ISABEL

What brings you back to me each night?

JESÚS

My feet?

ISABEL

I am serious.

JESÚS

Yo también hablo en serio.

ISABEL

Just your feet?

JESÚS

Is there a right answer?

ISABEL

Por supuesto.

JESÚS

My . . . my . . . my . . .

ISABEL

¿Sí?

JESÚS

. . . heart?

ISABEL

As the great Mexican philosopher said: Bingo!

JESÚS

I prefer Lotería.

ISABEL

Yo también.

JESÚS

Tengo una pregunta para ti.

ISABEL

What is your question?

JESÚS

What if I never came back . . . here, to you?

ISABEL

Maybe your life would be better.

JESÚS

No sé.

ISABEL

And maybe my life would be better.

JESÚS

No sé.

ISABEL

(Pause, both in thought. Then, jumping to her feet, ISABEL claps in excitement.)

Let us kill time!

JESÚS

Time will die without our help.

ISABEL

Let us play Piso and Afortunada! I will be Afortunada, you will be Piso.

JESÚS

¿Quiénes son?

ISABEL

You know, the two from yesterday!

(Clears throat, stands erect, holds up right index finger.)

Sisyphus Explains . . .

JESÚS

(Jumping to feet, excited.)

No, no, no, not that one! Do one about a cat! ¡Amo los poemas sobre gatos! Piso did not let Afortunada do a cat poem!

ISABEL

Ah, you *do* remember!

JESÚS

I remember nothing!

ISABEL

But you said . . .

JESÚS

I said nothing!

ISABEL

Ni modo. I will recite the poem . . .

(clearing throat)

They laugh
or cry
at my "plight"
that I need not
describe . . .

JESÚS

(Waving arms in front of ISABEL's face, agitated.)

¡No! Not the Sisyphus poem!

ISABEL

(Still trying to ignore JESÚS.)

But, in truth,
this is great pleasure . . .

JESÚS

(stomping feet)

¡No! ¡No! ¡No!

ISABEL

(Annoyed, turning to JESÚS, yelling.)

Quaquaquaqua!

JESÚS

(stomping feet)

¡No! ¡No! ¡No!

ISABEL

(yelling)

Quaquaquaqua!

JESÚS

(Sits on bench, holding head with both hands.)

I want to leave this place.

ISABEL

No, we must stay.

JESÚS

Stay? Why?

ISABEL

We must wait for Godínez.

JESÚS

¿Por qué?

ISABEL

(Sits next to JESÚS.)

You know why.

JESÚS

I do?

ISABEL

Yes.

JESÚS

Because we must?

ISABEL

Yes.

JESÚS

Because we have no choice?

ISABEL

Yes.

JESÚS

Because we must wait for Godínez?

ISABEL

Yes.

JESÚS

We must wait for Godínez.

ISABEL

Yes, we must wait for Godínez.

JESÚS

Yes, that is what I thought. Por supuesto.

ISABEL

Yes.

JESÚS

(JESÚS lies down, curls up, head on ISABEL's lap.)

I will sleep now.

ISABEL

(Placing hand on JESÚS's shoulder, slowly patting, as if calming a baby.)

Yes.

JESÚS

(Closes eyes.)

Estoy tan cansado.

ISABEL

(soothingly)

Yes, sleep.

JESÚS

Gracias, Chavalita.

ISABEL

Por nada.

JESÚS

Gracias.

(They remain silent, at peace, for a few moments.)

ISABEL

(Pensively, to herself.)

And so we will wait for Godínez. Maybe he will make things better, stop this cycle, stop the cages, keep you safe. Yes, we will wait for Godínez because we have no choice.

(pause)

Why does it happen, over and over and over? Why do they take you, my friend, and put you in a cage in the hopes of deporting you? What harm have you done to them? You are as much of this country as you are of México. But you are not home in either place. Ni de aquí, ni de allá.

(pause)

But what can I do? Each day, I promise to stay vigilant throughout the night, but I fail you, I fall asleep, I enter dreams of yesterday when we were happy and young. And in my slumber, they take you, put you in a cold cage. But those babosos forget to lock your cage and you escape, each night, and make your way back to me. But why? Are you an animal to be locked up in a cage? No. Or maybe yes. No. I do not know anymore.

(softly)

Híjole.

(Sighs, looks down at JESÚS.)

Maybe you should not return here. Perhaps tonight, after I fall asleep and they take you and throw you in that cage, you should make a different plan for your escape. Maybe there is a safe place, far from me, where you can live free from those monsters who want you out of this country. Why do you return to me? Why have you not learned? American dirt is a lie, not to be trusted. They use you when they need cheap work, then when they are done with you, they snatch you up in the middle of the night to rid themselves of your presence. ¡Ay Dios mío! Who gives them the right?

(pause)

Or maybe . . .

(Turns to look at tree branches.)

Maybe a bit of rope and that tree branch can help you escape this prison forever. It could be over so fast. No more cages, no more suffering, no more creeping back to this park to be with me. A nice, long rest.

(pause)

Or maybe . . . the rope is for me, not you. I could use a nice, long rest también.

(Mimics hanging herself, sticks out tongue, crosses eyes, sighs, drops arm.)

As the great Mexican artist said: I hope the exit is joyful and I hope never to return.

(sighs)

No, that bit of rope has a better use for you, Chuy, no? That makes the most sense. You are the one suffering each night without end. La cuerda es tuya.

(pause, thinking)

But what about me? I would be alone. Siempre. What about *me?*

(Turns to look at JESÚS, sighs.)

Maybe Godínez is the answer, not a bit of rope. We will wait for him. We have no choice.

JESÚS

(Stirs, mumbling in sleep.)

Mmmmmmmm . . . Godínez . . . mmmmmmm . . .

ISABEL

(Perks up.)

What is that? ¿Quién está ahí? Could that be Godínez?

JESÚS

(JESÚS's eyes pop open. He sits up.)

¿Qué?

PISO

(off)

Oh, what is time to me now? Pull me if you must, to where I do not know.

ISABEL

Piso and Afortunada! They are back!

(ISABEL jumps up, runs to middle of road to meet PISO and AFORTUNADA. JESUS is confused, remains seated, unexcited.)

PISO

(off)

Oh, where do we go, I do not know!

(PISO and AFORTUNADA enter stage right. AFORTUNADA pulls a beautiful, large, two-wheeled, wooden cart that is painted gold. In the cart sits PISO in a new wing-backed, upholstered chair, holding a glass of wine. They both wear the same outfit: black pants and short-sleeved guayaberas. Their clothes are clean. PISO's hair is still nicely cut and combed, but he wears a white bandana on his

eyes with blood stains where his eye sockets would be. AFORTUNADA's hair is now combed, neat. AFORTUNADA pulls the cart to center stage. ISABEL smiles in anticipation. JESÚS watches from the bench, confused.)

It is time to rest. Please stop here, Afortunada.

(AFORTUNADA stops.)

Thank you, you are too kind.

(PISO stands, unsteady, hands out because he cannot see.)

Please open.

(AFORTUNADA walks calmly to the little gate at the side of the cart, opens it, waits.)

Stepstool, please.

(AFORTUNADA reaches into the cart, pulls out a stepstool, places in front of the cart's door, offers PISO an arm. PISO reaches out, finds AFORTUNADA's arm, gingerly steps out of the cart, steps onto the ground carefully.)

JESÚS

(Stands, slowly walks to join ISABEL.)

Who are they?

ISABEL

You know . . .

JESÚS

I do not remember . . .

ISABEL

Piso and Afortunada!

JESÚS

Who?

ISABEL

The literary agent and his poet! From yesterday!

JESÚS

We know them?

ISABEL

¡Sí!

JESÚS

And this is a good thing?

ISABEL

¡Sí!

JESÚS

(getting excited)

¡Sí!

ISABEL

¡Sí!

JESÚS

(calming down, puzzled)

But what is wrong with Piso's eyes?

ISABEL

(Finally noticing PISO's bloody bandana, concerned.)

No sé.

PISO

(Steps back, a little frightened.)

Who? What?

ISABEL

Welcome back, Señor Piso Mojado!

PISO

Who is shouting at me? Please stop!

(covering ears)

Are you unable to see that I am blind! A blind man's hearing is amplified by his blindness, transforming a mere whisper into an intolerable cacophony!

JESÚS

(shouting)

Who . . .

(PISO jumps in pain at JESÚS's voice, JESÚS now whispers.)

Who is this blind man?

PISO

(Gaining composure, extends his right hand toward JESÚS, searches for JESÚS's hand. JESÚS smiles, takes PISO's hand, and they start to shake hands slowly.)

My name is Piso . . .

JESÚS

(JESÚS's smile disappears, pulls hand away.)

Piso? That is a low name!

ISABEL

No, Chuy, this is the great literary agent Piso!

(PISO smiles, nods.)

We encountered him and his poet yesterday at this same spot. You do not remember, Chuy?

JESÚS

I do not remember. And I did not like the poem his poet recited to us.

ISABEL

Then you *do* remember!

JESÚS

Do not tell me what is in my head!

PISO

(Puzzled, tries again, this time extending his hand toward ISABEL's voice. She takes his hand, and they start to shake.)

At your service. I am Señor Piso Mojado.

JESÚS

(JESÚS walks over to AFORTUNADA, looks her up and down, curious.)

¿Te conozco?

PISO

(Letting go of ISABEL's hand.)

Gentlepeople, may I introduce you to Afortunada, one of the greatest novelists of our time . . . and my newest client.

(AFORTUNADA puffs out chest proudly. ISABEL and JESÚS look at each other, puzzled.)

ISABEL

(Turning to PISO.)

No, this is Afortunada, your *poet*, not novelist.

JESÚS

She recited a poem for us yesterday: the one about that pendejo who pushes that pinche boulder up the hill . . .

(Mimes pushing a boulder.)

. . . but I wanted un poema sobre un gato.

(Mimes holding a cat and petting it.)

ISABEL

Yes, this is the same poet we met yesterday.

JESÚS

Sí, la misma persona.

PISO

Do you mock a blind man? I know who my client is! She is the newest literary star, and she signed with me this morning. Afortunada is a brilliant novelist, a wordsmith of the highest caliber. I do not waste my time with poets who only bring misery and unpaid bills. And most of them are drug addicts and drunkards, to be quite frank with you. No poets for me! Give me a novelist any day.

ISABEL

What happened to your eyes, if I may ask?

JESÚS

¿Estás bien?

PISO

(calmly, matter-of-factly)

Gentlepeople, Afortunada blinded me with a pen.

JESÚS

¡Qué horrible!

ISABEL

What? Why have you not prosecuted her? What have the authorities said about this horrible crime?

PISO

(proudly)

I am a literary agent. Afortunada is my client. And she will be a bestseller! I—we—will be wealthy beyond our imaginations! What is the loss of my eyes when I will live in comfort for the rest of my life?

ISABEL

(shocked, softly)

Híjole.

JESÚS

(shocked, softly)

Sí. Híjole.

ISABEL

She did it with a pen?

PISO

Yes.

JESÚS

¿Qué tipo de pluma era?

ISABEL

Yes, what kind of pen was it?

PISO

I do not know. Perhaps a fountain pen. I cannot remember!

JESÚS

¿Cómo podría no saber qué tipo de pluma era?

ISABEL

Yes, I would have remembered what kind of pen Chuy used to blind me.

JESÚS

(Turning to ISABEL, insulted.)

I never would have blinded you!

ISABEL

I know, I know, Chuy.

JESÚS

I have wanted to kill you, por supuesto, but I would never think of blinding you.

PISO

(Shaking head, not believing the stupid banter.)

Talking about it will not bring back my eyes. No. It does not matter. What does matter is that I have a brilliant novelist as a client who, no doubt, will bring me—us—wealth and fame. What more could a literary agent desire?

AFORTUNADA

(shouting)

Allegory!

(Startled, ISABEL and JESÚS run back to park bench, sit, and hold each other in fear.)

Conflict!

(ISABEL and JESÚS shake in fear, hug each other tighter.)

Irony!
Exposition!
Dénouement!
Foreshadowing!

(pauses for emphasis)

Freytag's Pyramid!

PISO

(Searches for AFORTUNADA's shoulder, finds it, gently places hand on her shoulder.)

Please save your creative energies.

AFORTUNADA

(Turns to PISO, uncertain, whispers.)

Climax?

PISO

Perfect. No more please.

(Removes hand from AFORTUNADA's shoulder, explains to ISABEL and JESÚS.)

No need to be afraid, gentlepeople. The novelist has the tools of her trade as does the poet, but with one difference.

ISABEL

And what is that difference?

PISO

The novelist's tools bring in much more in the way of financial remuneration, of course.

ISABEL

(Releases JESÚS, nodding.)

Of course.

JESÚS

Por supuesto.

PISO

Would you like to hear my great author recite from her novel in progress—gratis?

ISABEL

Free is good.

JESÚS

Something about gatos!

PISO

A true coincidence, gentlepeople! The great novelist's latest work does have a character whose nickname is "Kitten." A truly remarkable stroke of luck.

JESÚS

Close enough.

ISABEL

Yes! That would be a pretty way to spend time as we wait for Godínez!

JESÚS

(Turning to ISABEL.)

Who is Godínez?

ISABEL

We are waiting for Godínez!

JESÚS

Sí, sí. Estamos esperando a Godínez.

PISO

Yes, yes, we may have my novelist recite a few pretty words. Why not?

(Pointing to stepstool.)

Afortunada, prepare to orate!

(AFORTUNADA smiles, steps onto the stool, faces audience, clears throat.)

Please recite an excerpt from your novel in progress, *Sanctity*.

ISABEL

A mysterious title. It must be brilliant! Let us hear the excerpt.

PISO

Very well. Gentlepeople, I give you the great novelist, Joshua Franklin!

JESÚS AND ISABEL

¿Quién?

PISO

I said, Joshua Franklin. That is Afortunada's nom de plume.

ISABEL

What?

PISO

That is her pen name. I learned long ago that selling books is a business with certain rules. Rule number one: For a book to sell, it must be reviewed. And a book written by a person named Afortunada will not attract reviewers from the major publications—the literary intelligentsia, if you will. However, a major novel by an author with a name like Joshua Franklin will be reviewed.

(Turning to AFORTUNADA.)

Joshua Franklin, recite an excerpt from *Sanctity*.

AFORTUNADA

(Clears throat, holds up right index finger, recites in dramatic voice.)

From the novel *Sanctity* by Joshua Franklin. Chapter 1: Sanctity in Trouble.

"Oh kitten, I'm delighted you called," the girl's aunt said on the telephone. "I am not well. At times I believe my life consists of nothing more than my body plotting against me with a plan of torture that gets more devious each day."

"How is that different from my life?" the girl, Hap, said. It was now her habit to call her aunt midway through her dinner break at the Red Lobster. She had many thoughts about her job—which was far beneath her desires and abilities—but Hap put on a brave face for her aunt, and these phone calls gave her a chance to have an obligatory conversation without saying too much and the honest opportunity to end the conversation because her manager needed her to get back to waiting tables.

"I am seeing double again," her aunt explained. "It's like my world has been split in two, like a teensy French chef has sliced my vision with a very sharp knife or something."

(Dropping right arm, AFORTUNADA steps off stool, bows head, waits.)

ISABEL

(clapping)

Wonderful!

JESÚS

(clapping)

¡Otro!

ISABEL

(Clapping slows, stops, suddenly pensive.)

But what did it mean?

JESÚS

Are we to be impressed?

PISO

Does it matter? They are just words organized into lines and paragraphs and chapters. Why should it mean anything? And were you not riveted? Such simple language creating such complex characters, so real you could almost smell their perfume. But in the end, the real question is: Will *Sanctity* by Joshua Franklin sell? And I have little doubt it will because the critics will not ignore it.

ISABEL AND JESÚS

(ISABEL and JESÚS look at each other, shrug, turn back to PISO.)

You are the expert.

PISO

Well, I certainly am.

JESÚS

(Begging, rubbing stomach.)

By the way, do you have a mango that you can spare for poor, hungry Chuy?

PISO

(PISO reaches for Afortunada's arm, feels for stool with right foot, steps onto stool and into cart.)

No time for mangos, gentlepeople, though I have many here in this lunch basket.

(JESÚS is distraught.)

PISO

Off to the city to meet with publishers!

(AFORTUNADA gets in front of cart, grabs handles, and starts to pull.)

JESÚS

¡No!

PISO

Adieu, gentlepeople! We will never see each other again, no doubt, but wish me well in my endeavors. Faster, please, Afortunada! Faster!

(PISO and AFORTUNADA exit.)

ISABEL

¡No!

PISO

(off)

Faster, please, my great novelist!

ISABEL

They are gone forever.

JESÚS

I am unhappy.

ISABEL

(laughs)

JESÚS

Why do you laugh at my unhappiness?

ISABEL

As the great Mexican playwright said: Nothing is funnier than unhappiness.

JESÚS

How will we pass the time as we wait for—¿Cúal es su nombre? Ah! Sí. Godínez!

ISABEL

A game to end our boredom! I will say a word. You must respond with another word. A word that naturally follows.

JESÚS

What kind of word?

ISABEL

(Thinks, smiling mischievously.)

Aguascalientes!

JESÚS

(Thinks a moment, smiles, claps once, understanding game.)

Baja California!

ISABEL

Baja California Sur!

(With the naming of each Mexican state and the federal district, ISABEL and JESÚS get more dramatic and joyful, dancing or squirming or mugging with each pronouncement.)

JESÚS

Campeche!

ISABEL

Coahuila!

JESÚS

Colima!

ISABEL

Chiapas!

JESÚS

Chihuahua!

ISABEL

Ciudad de México!

JESÚS

Durango!

ISABEL

Guanajuato!

JESÚS

Guerrero!

ISABEL

Hidalgo!

JESÚS

Jalisco!

ISABEL

México!

JESÚS

Michoacán!

ISABEL

Morelos!

JESÚS

Nayarit!

ISABEL

Nuevo León!

JESÚS

Oaxaca!

ISABEL

Puebla!

JESÚS

Querétaro!

ISABEL

Quintana Roo!

JESÚS

San Luis Potosí!

ISABEL

Sinaloa!

JESÚS

Sonora!

ISABEL

Tabasco!

JESÚS

Tamaulipas!

ISABEL

Tlaxcala!

JESÚS

Veracruz!

ISABEL

Yucatán!

JESÚS

Zacatecas!

(ISABEL and JESÚS proudly clap, dance a little dance, smile, mug, exhausted, pleased with themselves. They eventually tire.)

ISABEL

That is my favorite game!

JESÚS

Yo también. Have you been to all those places?

ISABEL

No, Chuy, you know that. I have another twelve states to visit, then I will have seen them all.

JESÚS

May I go with you?

ISABEL

Of course, Chuy! I could never go without you.

(JESÚS walks toward the bench.)

Where are you going?

JESÚS

(Stops, pauses, mischievous smile appears on his face.)

Barcelona.

ISABEL

Oh.

JESÚS

Not Barcelona. To this bench. That is where I am going. Estoy tan cansado.

(JESÚS yawns, climbs onto bench, curls up to nap, closes eyes.)

ISABEL

Sleep, my old friend.

(Walking downstage, looks at tree, pensive, talking to herself.)

We must be ready to meet Godínez. And should he arrive while you sleep, I promise that I will wake you. As the great Mexican philosopher said: Sleeping is the best way to pass the time while you wait for the important thing to happen.

(pause)

We will meet Godínez here, together, by this tree, and he will . . . he will . . . ay! I do not know what Godínez will do or say, but we must wait to meet him, then he will let us know. I am sure of it. I am sure of it.

(Turning to JESÚS, who sleeps.)

CHILD

(off)

Mr. Albert?

(enters)

Mr. Albert?

(Stopping in front of ISABEL, who looks down at CHILD.)

ISABEL

Why do you still call me Mr. Albert?

CHILD

Are you Mr. Albert?

ISABEL

As I told you yesterday, I am Isabel, and my close friends call me Chavalita. But you may call me Señora Soledad out of respect for my age and station. Who is it you are looking for? Are you the child who came yesterday with the news that Señor Godínez wanted us to wait for him by this tree?

CHILD

No, Señora Soledad. That was not me. Maybe it was my twin.

ISABEL

You both work at the bicycle repair shop for Señor Godínez, correct?

CHILD

Sí, Señora Soledad.

ISABEL

Which one are you?

CHILD

What do you mean, Señora Soledad?

ISABEL

Are you the boy or the girl? Yesterday, your twin did not know.

CHILD

And I do not know, Señora Soledad.

ISABEL

You must know. Someone must know.

CHILD

No, Señora Soledad. I do not know.

ISABEL

Ni modo. You are the twin that Señor Godínez beats, correct?

CHILD

He does not beat my twin, Señora Soledad.

ISABEL

Ah! So perhaps you are the boy? Maybe Señor Godínez is a man of the old ways and would only beat a boy?

CHILD

I do not know, Señora Soledad.

ISABEL

(Thinking in silence, then gets an idea.)

You are very thin, just like your twin. Are you hungry, child?

CHILD

Sí, Señora Soledad.

ISABEL

(Searching pockets, finds mango, presents it to CHILD.)

Here, child, a delicious, ripe mango for you. Take it.

CHILD

(Taking mango in both hands.)

Gracias, Señora Soledad.

ISABEL

Por nada.

(pauses, thoughtful)

Child, were you born in México?

CHILD

Sí, Señora Soledad.

ISABEL

Do you know which state?

CHILD

Sí, Señora Soledad.

ISABEL

Which one?

CHILD

Oaxaca, Señora Soledad.

ISABEL

That is a fine state.

CHILD

I do not know, Señora Soledad.

ISABEL

Trust me, child, it is a fine state. Do you know which state I was born in?

CHILD

No, Señora Soledad.

ISABEL

Of course you do not know. Why should you? We are strangers to each other, no? So I will tell you: I was born in the great state of Chihuahua.

CHILD

(Points to the sleeping JESÚS.)

And what state was he born in, Señora Soledad?

ISABEL

(chuckles)

Jesús? He was born in Texas. El Paso, to be exact.

CHILD

(puzzled)

Is that in México, Señora Soledad?

ISABEL

No, it is part of this country . . .

(Gesturing around herself.)

in the United States. Texas was once part of México, long ago. Anyway, my friend over there . . .

(Gesturing to JESÚS.)

. . . never remembers that he was born in the United States, that he is a citizen of this country—*our* country. He lost his birth certificate long ago and never remembers that he needs to get another copy.

CHILD

(Nods silently.)

Why do you not remind him, Señora Soledad?

ISABEL

(Puzzled, then defensive.)

I always forget. Do you blame me, child?

CHILD

No, Señora Soledad.

ISABEL

I assume you have a message for me from Señor Godínez?

CHILD

Sí, Señora Soledad.

ISABEL

And what is that message?

CHILD

Señor Godínez says that he cannot come this evening, but he hopes to come tomorrow.

ISABEL

This is the same message your twin gave me yesterday. We have been waiting for him for two, three, maybe four days, I do not remember. What of that? Does our waiting not matter to Señor Godínez?

CHILD

I do not know, Señora Soledad.

ISABEL

Well, tomorrow it must be. We have no choice, do we? You may go now, child.

CHILD

But Señora Soledad . . .

ISABEL

What is it, child?

CHILD

What should I tell Señor Godínez?

ISABEL

(Scratching chin, thinking.)

Tell him you met me, we spoke, I fed you just as I fed your twin yesterday, and I sent you off. Can you do that, child?

CHILD

Sí, Señora Soledad.

(CHILD hesitates, turns, starts to walk, turns to look at ISABEL one last time, then runs off. Suddenly, sky goes dark. It is now a dark night. Moon rises into the middle of the sky.)

ISABEL

(ISABEL looks up to the moon and addresses it.)

You have returned. It is good to see you again. Have you missed me? Yes, of course you have. How could you not?

(Puts hand to ear to hear better.)

¿Cómo?

(Nods, drops hand.)

Of course I appreciate your visits. And I will mourn the day you stop.

JESÚS

(Stirring, eyes still closed.)

Chavalita? ¿Dónde estás?

ISABEL

(To the moon.)

Lo siento. My friend needs me. Thank you for visiting.

JESÚS

(Stirring, eyes still closed.)

Chavalita? Who are you talking to? Where are you?

ISABEL

(Looks toward JESÚS, starts to walk to him.)

Estoy aquí.

(Standing in front of bench, looking down.)

Estoy aquí, Chuy.

(Bending over, ISABEL lifts JESÚS's head, sits, gingerly puts JESÚS's head on her lap.)

JESÚS

(Eyes still closed, sighing.)

I had a dream, Chavalita. You fell asleep here next to me and they came and took me again and put me in that cold cage. All because you fell asleep and did not fight them off.

ISABEL

(Slowly patting JESÚS's arm to soothe him.)

It was only a dream, my friend. I will protect you, Chuy. I will keep you safe. No te estoy mintiendo. I will stay alert all night.

(pause)

Do not worry, my old friend. I will never betray you.

(pause)

You have my word.

JESÚS

Mil gracias.

ISABEL

Por nada.

JESÚS

Tengo hambre. Do you have a mango?

ISABEL

No, Chuy. I gave you the last one yesterday. I have had nothing in my pockets all day. I would never lie to you.

JESÚS

Oh, yes, you said that.

ISABEL

But I hope that tomorrow I will have a mango. And if I do, I promise to give it to you and to no one else.

JESÚS

Sí. Mañana.

(pause)

Talk to me, Chavalita.

ISABEL

About what, my friend?

JESÚS

Tell me about your life.

ISABEL

What do you want to know, my friend?

JESÚS

(pause, thinking)

Did you ever marry?

ISABEL

(smiles)

Oh, yes, I had a big wedding when I was young. You were there.

JESÚS

I was?

ISABEL

Sí. You do not remember?

JESÚS

(pause)

Tell me about your wedding. Who did you marry?

ISABEL

(Pained look as memories return.)

Who did I marry?

JESÚS

Sí. Who did you marry?

ISABEL

(Relenting to the truth, softly.)

I married your brother, Nacho. You do not remember?

JESÚS

Ah, sí, sí, Nacho. And was it a beautiful wedding?

ISABEL

Yes, it was beautiful.

JESÚS

And did you have children?

ISABEL

Sí.

JESÚS

How many?

ISABEL

Two—a boy and a girl.

(Pause, thoughtful, trying to remember, then remembering, a chasm of sorrow.)

Twins.

JESÚS

Ah, sí, sí, twins. And where is Nacho?

ISABEL

(pause, thinking, puzzled)

I do not know.

JESÚS

And where are the twins?

ISABEL

(sighs)

I do not know.

JESÚS

(pause, thinking)

And tell me, Chavalita: Did I ever marry?

ISABEL

No, Chuy. You never married.

JESÚS

¿Por qué no?

ISABEL

You said the best person was already taken.

JESÚS

Ah, sí, sí. And who was already taken?

ISABEL

I do not know.

JESÚS

(pause)

But I am not alone.

ISABEL

No.

JESÚS

You are here.

ISABEL

Yes, my friend, I am here.

JESÚS

Siempre estarás aquí conmigo.

ISABEL

Sí, sí. I will always be with you.

JESÚS

Gracias, Chavalita.

ISABEL

In the meantime, I will stay alert. As always, I will stay awake all night to protect you, my old friend. You have nothing to fear while I am by your side. I will never forget my old friend.

JESÚS

Gracias, Chavalita.

ISABEL

I will protect you, as always.

JESÚS

Gracias, Chavalita.

ISABEL

No one will take you tonight, I promise.

JESÚS

Gracias, Chavalita.

ISABEL

You are my friend.

JESÚS

Gracias, Chavalita.

ISABEL

You may trust me.

JESÚS

Gracias, Chavalita.

ISABEL

I would never lie to you.

JESÚS

Gracias, Chavalita.

ISABEL

Te prometo. A promise from me is as good as gold.

JESÚS

Gracias, Chavalita.

(Both grow quiet. ISABEL's eyes start to flutter. She slowly nods off. Both are now asleep. Tableau.)

(CURTAIN, END OF PLAY.)

ACKNOWLEDGMENTS

The following portions of this book were previously published and are reprinted here with permission:

Preface: First published in the *Daily Journal* in a slightly different form under the title "An Absurd Stalemate on Immigration Reform." Copyright © 2023 by Daniel A. Olivas. Reprinted by permission of the author.

"Sisyphus Explains": First published in the online literary journal *The Poetry Victims* (2005); featured in *Crossing the Border: Collected Poems* (Regal House, 2017). Copyright © 2005 by Daniel A. Olivas. Reprinted by permission of the author.

As I often have observed, giving thanks is fraught with peril because it is impossible to list every person who played a role in bringing a book into the world. But I hope that I have, over the years, personally thanked those who have been supportive of me and my unfathomable vocation that we call the writing life. So here are some thoughts on gratitude that will be inadequate and imperfect.

Mil gracias to those passionate, remarkable, and talented directors, actors, and other theater makers who brilliantly brought this play to life in readings and for the stage. I specifically and proudly acknowledge your theaters and many of you at the beginning of this book.

I am grateful to the wonderful people at the University of New Mexico Press. Your consideration, passion, and support are all any writer could want. I have been a fan of your books for many years, and now I can proudly proclaim that I am a member of your publishing family!

I offer a big, virtual, Chicano abrazo to the many extraordinary and devoted writers who have encouraged and inspired my literary life. And as I have done on many occasions, I offer additional thanks to my fellow bloggers at the online literary site *La Bloga*.

As for my day job, I offer thanks to my friends at the California Department of Justice who have read my books and attended my various book readings. You continue to help me integrate my life as a lawyer with that of an author.

I thank my parents, who always made certain that we were a family of books and that we each became proud holders of library cards. You taught your children to love and appreciate our Mexican culture and roots as well as art in all its forms. You also introduced us to the theater by tuning into plays and musicals that appeared on television, taking us to movie theaters to gawk at the splendor of filmed musicals, as well as purchasing play tickets for us even when money was tight. I offer a special acknowledgment to my late father, who had unfulfilled dreams of becoming a published writer. This is now my third book to be released since you were called back, but I feel your love and support with every word I write. I miss you dearly, Pop.

Finally, I thank my wife, Susan Formaker, and our son, Benjamin Formaker-Olivas. As I have said many times before, I am nothing without you. You give me joy and you fill my life with so much happiness. I love you both with all of my Chicano heart. I hope that you enjoy my new book.

ABOUT THE AUTHOR

DANIEL A. OLIVAS, the grandson of Mexican immigrants, was born and raised near downtown Los Angeles. He received his degree in English literature from Stanford University and his law degree from UCLA. Olivas is an award-winning author of fiction, nonfiction, plays, and poetry, including *Chicano Frankenstein: A Novel* (2024), *My Chicano Heart: New and Collected Stories of Love and Other Transgressions* (2024), *How to Date a Flying Mexican: New and Collected Stories* (2022), and *Crossing the Border: Collected Poems* (2017). Widely anthologized, he has written on culture and literature for *The New York Times, Los Angeles Review of Books, Los Angeles Times, Alta Journal, Jewish Journal, Latino Book Review, Zócalo,* and *The Guardian*. He writes regularly for *La Bloga*, a site dedicated to Latinx literature and the arts.